They Thought They Could Bury Us.... But They Didn't Know We Were Seeds

Lisa Helms

BookLeaf Publishing

Presentation by *BookLeaf Publishing*

Web: www.bookleafpub.com

E-mail: info@bookleafpub.com

ISBN: 9789357745116

First edition 2023

This book is dedicated to anyone in the world who experiences any range of debilitating mental health challenges or any sort of disability. Something I've learned from my time as a mental health/disability advocate, is that disability is a natural part of the human experience. So, there aren't many, if any at all, people who wouldn't be included in this dedication.

As a whole, the world needs more love and understanding. In writing this book, I hope to bring a voice to the neuro-divergent, neuro-atypical, misfits who may find it in their hands. I hope when people read these words, they feel their worth, and they feel they have a voice. All I've ever wanted is to share my thoughts with those who feel less than or alone, as well as those who feel they fit in most spaces. My hope is that it will bring strength to those who feel "othered" and perspective to those who feel on a larger level, included.

ACKNOWLEDGEMENT

My family, Mom, Dad, my brother Michael, and my sister Nikki, especially, are who I would like to acknowledge with the writing of my first book of poetry. Their constant encouragement and support are one major reason I am able to get up and do what I do every day.

Mom, where to begin? One thing I've never been confused about in my life is how wanted I am by you. You make this abundantly clear every chance you get. You answer every phone call and return every call you miss. You drive me places when I'm not well, even if it's far out of your way. You still make us Easter baskets and make every birthday and holiday special, and for this, I cannot thank you enough.

I wouldn't be the person I am today without my dad. Dad, every groan-worthy, knee-slapping joke I know I learned from you. Not only this, but one of my favorite pictures of us was of a Father, Daughter dance from when I was a kid. I cherish this memory, along with so many others. Throughout the years, you've been there. Maybe you weren't perfect, but you were there, and I can't tell you enough how much you are loved and appreciated.

My relationship with my brother, Michael, is unbreakable. He's my inspiration when I feel like I can't get out of bed. You know the challenges I face, and I know the challenges you face; every day we walk through this life together is a day worth living. Thank you for every lofi music video you find and send me to make my workdays that much more bearable. Being your big sister is the greatest honor I know.

Dearest Nikki, my beautiful sister, you have shaped who I am as a person more than words can describe. From singing lullabies to you until you fell asleep as a child, to driving and singing in the car with you, our memories keep me smiling. The song you leave in my heart keeps my heart beating and my feet moving, even when I feel like giving up. Thank you for our sisterhood.

I can't forget my closest friends, Evan Izi, Charlia, Sam and Arica.

Evan, Izi, Charlia, going through high school with you is definitely the only way I survived.

We survived together. The fact that our friendships are still as strong as they were back then, restores my faith in this life. Evan, I love that we live close enough to watch the Simpsons or go out to brunch any day we wish. Izi and Charlia, I come to visit as often as possible, but our phone calls carry me through until I can catch the next plane.

Sam and I are more recent friends who have known each other for a while now. Our friendship is so special to me. We are mental health warriors and totally badass for making it through each day with the gusto we give the world. Your words of encouragement throughout each day keep me sane and give me something to look forward to. Even a simple voice clip from you makes me smile instantly.

Arica, my lovely friend, what would I do without our daily Snapchat conversations? We have by far my longest-standing Snapchat streak at a whopping 500+ days! Our friendship goes far beyond Snapchat, however. You are the first person I think of to call when I need someone to watch Vince, and I'm more than willing to come to help you with Mau if you go on a trip. As cat moms, we both know how much trust it takes to leave our babies with another person for any stretch of time. Also, as artists, we gain inspiration from each other and cheer each other on, and this has been invaluable to my growth.

PREFACE

I chose to write about mental health, as it is a topic that can cover so many different aspects of life. Every person experiences mental health, whether it be a positive, negative, scary or calm experience, and it can change in a split second and from day to day.

My own journey with mental health started at the age of 14. You can imagine how arduous of a journey that was for my family and me. From the first time I was hospitalized, to being diagnosed with Bipolar Disorder, to living life as a now 30-something, I have encountered myriad twists and turns.

It has been a huge goal of mine to share my mental health story with people in an accessible and relatable way. I want to share my story in a way that helps people know they're not alone. No matter what your mental health challenges bring you day to day, someone out there is going through something similar. I have found success in my mental health goals, as well as downfalls like relapse and repeated hospitalizations.

All of this is to say, I live each day to the fullest. When I saw the ad for the 21-Day Poetry Challenge and saw I had an opportunity at my fingertips to publish my first book, I seized the moment. I didn't have much time, as it was the last day to sign up when I joined the challenge. I decided not to let this adventure slip through my fingers.

My Mind, My Castle

My mind is my castle
A castle with never-ending amounts
Of doors
And that sounds overwhelming
But, it's just so comforting
To know every day I'll discover new treasures
About myself

To know every day I'll close some doors
And open some more

I take control

Only I know my way
In and out of the rooms
If I have memories
With or of a person
And I need them to
Leave my life
I simply close the door
And lock it
And open it again
When I'm feeling sentimental
Or I need to look back on
What they taught me

Don't worry—
I leave food and water for them

These rooms in my castle
Are magical
It's like one big
Expansive
Room of Requirement
It takes the form of a
Majestic home
For my experiences
For my thoughts
For my spirit to
Roam free

The library
Full of essays I've lost from
High school
Full to the brim of lost poetry
I never had the nerve to write down
Full of the ones I did have the nerve to.

It's a mysterious, wonderful,
Sometimes scary place.
But it's all mine. I think I'll keep it.

XX Large Woman

I'm a
Large
Woman
And I'm becoming more and more
Aware and okay with this
Every second of every day
Here are some foods I feed myself
As sloppily as I please

Bacon, Chocolate, peach rings,
Chicken wings and all the
Give-of-no-fucks I can manage

Here's why the media ain't shit and
My body is beautiful and
Always changing
Much like my mind

XXX-Large to be exact
Or at least that's what my
T-shirt tag says
But this label is no longer
Applicable when we talk about
My heart

Yes, most of my energy goes to
Loving everything and everyone
People,
People like certain politicians and
Stockbrokers and bankers and
Average Joes never think about

People of all colors, abilities and sizes
I do this because I know for a
Fact I haven't been shown the same
But like my grandmother always
Taught me-- leave the world
Better than how it came--
And I respect my elders

Wings

I have a story similar to Maleficent
We loved each other as children love
When we grew—he, a proprietor of the
patriarchy—
Me, a beneficiary of disadvantage
Of fighting for the right to my body
We grew in to the roles laid out
For us.

He licking his fingers with greed
Me aiming to catch mere scraps of hope
Thirsty for the hydration of being
Treated as a good investment
To be seen and appreciated
To be
Respected

Despite the system's need to
Strip me
Of my identity I KNEW who
Me
Was

I had to re-learn that, though,
When trust was granted to a thief

He took it without permission
Started a pattern of hiding behind
Drapes of shame
I shattered to pieces
Realized I couldn't be fixed by
Glue and tape
Squished me like a grape
Under his shoe
Before I could realize I'm
Really a fine wine

A pattern of not speaking when
I wanted to scream
Now I'm needing to re-learn
How to let the safe people
Not sure I trust I know how to pick these
Few out of the many

He stole my wings
But I've begun to reclaim
What's mine
I'm finding my wings again

Time

All there is, is Time
We have, at the same Time

All the Time in the world
And absolutely no Time to speak of

At the same

Time

Tears

The tears streaming down my face
Have been like
Chinese water torture
Dripping, dripping down my
Face
All the way to my heart
Each one
Reminder after reminder
Of your touch
Long gone
Over time
They create a hold

This hold
Curses me into
Only wanting to lay in my bed
And handing my
Heart and my happiness over
To the first person who asks

I know that's not a way
To fill it

So, yes, it's a curse—
It's also a blessing

I'll find someone
Who's appreciation
Will not only
Fill the grave with
Fertile soil
And grow new Life
But will envelope me in Love
Their appreciation for my
Gift of true partnership
Will carry me through
The tears

The sunshine will return
To my eyes

I realize now
The true torture is
Not appreciating
Not respecting myself

My tears lately
Have been able to fill a whole lake
Like a mirror
My feelings for myself
Like a mirror
And the people I share
Love with
Reflect on what I think I deserve

I deserve to be loved
Because that's what I
Strive to share with the
World

I want someone who's
Not afraid to hold my hand
I deserve them

My body, and my mind, and my soul
Deserve respect
And health
And prosperity

Let's start reflecting

To My Mother

Mama,
If ever you worry
That you haven't taught me
All that you could have as well as
You could have

I'm writing to tell you
You've taught me a Louvre's worth of
Lessons and experiences

That when I make a mistake
There's no judgment between
You and I
Just the two of us
Building castles in the sky

That I don't have to
Let the past haunt me

That sometimes as
Women with a troubled past
That sometimes
We'll take the hard stuff out
On the people we love most
They'll forgive us anyway

You've taught me the
Importance of family
That this word is
Synonymous with
Forgiveness
Unconditional love
And ultimate security

That respect for my elders
Is more valuable than any silver or gold
That I will regret it if I don't
Because even if I know
More than them about some things
Time has taught them things that
Youth can't
And it's just the right thing to do

To always do the right thing
Even if it's not the easiest thing
That it usually isn't

That nothing I confess
Can make you Love me less

You're the first person I've loved
Who I've ever had "a song" with
When I hear it
I cry every time

You've taught me that
If I ever have a child
It's important for me to
Tell them the same thing
And to show them it's true

That respecting myself
Is the first step
To finding real love

That it's not the
Greatest idea
To find love in a bar
That with real love
I won't expect it when it shows up
To not rush the process

That Life is a gauntlet at times
And sometimes easy breezy
And full of butterfly kisses
And laughter
And freshly squeezed lemonade

That it's okay to pinch pennies
And that it's also important
To go out dancing sometimes

Basically, mama,

If I went through what you did,
I don't know that I'd have made it
Through

I don't think I'll fully understand
The magnitude to which you
Raise me up
Until I inevitably
Lose you
I wish that day
Never needed to come

But I'll remember all the times I
Laughed and cried and
Lived Life with you

You were my first friend
You gave me Life
No diamond will ever replace your love

Although
Someday when there is maybe
A ring on my left ring finger
I hope to God you're there
Because I'll need you to hold me
When I'm scared
And if there's
Some kind of wedding catastrophe
I'll need your street smarts and resourcefulness

To smooth it over

To Love Life
And all the beauty that it has to offer

Thank you forever
For sitting through
Every choir concert, doctor's appointment,
From trauma after
Trauma

Thanks for loving me
Before I was even born
If all we need is Love
I'm set for Life

Thanks doesn't even begin to say it

Radical

I've come to learn
To be unafraid
To be radical

To raise my voice
For injustice anywhere is
A threat
To justice
Everywhere

To plant seeds of change
So my kids can sit in the shade
And they'll do the same
And pretty soon we'll have a
Chain of change that can
Wrap around the earth
And the ozone layer will be
Repaired with the Love
That emanates from
The chain
We'll be able to breath again

Little Brother

Little brother
When did the time come
When you grew taller
Than me?
Because I used to carry you around
And when we played
You didn't have to be so
Conscious of how gentle you were being
I know that can be hard
But it's a non-issue
I'm so overjoyed
I tell it on the mountains
That it's okay for me to hug you now
Because that wasn't always the case

It used to be that
Anything that involved
Touch or wetness or texture
Wasn't doable without
A lot more effort than what I
Needed to put into doing
The same things
I know you and I were
Built differently

Every word you couldn't speak then
Was an IOU
For today when you can't
Get enough of language
And we look forward to
Conversations together
Even if it's just
"I love you, I love you too"

These words between me and you
Are what I live for

Perception

Having the best day
Of your Life
Is usually, logistically, an easy thing
To do

No matter what comes to you
You can remember what you
Believe in and stand for
And use it for support.

If you don't stand for
Something
You accept everything
The negative needs to be
Weeded out
To succeed

If you don't stand for
Something
Today is a great place to
State your case.
To begin to see Life
Through new eyes

And to have the best day
Of your life

Every Little Thing

Three little birds
Have been faithful
In reassuring me
And reassuring me and
Reassuring me time and again
That every little thing
Will be alright

I'm beginning the path
To believing them
To live a Life free of
Hesitation
So there's no regret over
What I didn't do

A Life full of Love
And good intentions and
Sorrys and moving on
Because I'm human
So I'll make mistakes
But when I do
Guilt doesn't help me or you

I'm human and so are you
And we're fucking this world up together

But Bob Marley calls on the
Birds to
Reassure us of one thing
Every little thing
Is gonna be alright

I just want everyone to
Feel loved
I just want for no one
To feel alone

How many people are on this
Earth
We may need to make
Some groups of there in a
World full of exclusive groups of two
But let's suck it up
Yes every little thing will
Be alright
But we have to
Share the weight of
Making it alright
Before the birds' wings break
And our sky-flyers
Die

And where would we be?
Bob Marley
Wouldn't be a legend

And my poetry would have
Ended before it started

Understand

Most of the Time
I'm okay with the way
Of the passing of Time
How sometimes it goes
Slow and other times
Rapid like the beating
Of my heart when I see you

I counted down the minutes
And hours until I could
See your face
Hear your voice
I don't think it'd
Be appropriate to
Touch your hands
Because there's
Someone else now

I'm really sorry for
How I treated you for
How I handled things
So I understand if you
Don't have the same enthusiasm
I do to see you

To Sister

Sitting, writing my feelings
Listening to NF with my sister
What would I do without her?
Probably waste away
Probably run away for days
Probably go missing from
Running non-stop from my
Problems
Problem is, she knows exactly
When I'm suffering
Knows exactly when I've reached
The point of no return
The point where I can no longer
Stifle my tears and hide from her

Thinking
Dreaming
Imagining a future
Without all the bullshit
I go through with my mental
Health not being where I want
It to be
How do I wake up
In the morning
Pry myself from my bed

As if my limbs are nailed down
As if my body is full of dead weight

Maybe would feel better if I
Just didn't feel anymore
If I just didn't exist anymore
Then I think

Who will protect them?
My family and friends
Who've always had my back
Always will
Always be looking out for me

These moments of darkness are like
Jumping into a vast ocean
Diving deep into the dark void
Realizing the moment I'm too
Far down to get back up in time
Do I give up or pray to Higher Power for the
Strength to swim to the surface
Fight for my life? Or Give this up?

Poem to, "Episode Me"

You're not just an
Episode to me
Because,
Being a separate
Entity
Would mean you're
Not a part of me?
How so
When I go
Everywhere in my mind
In every given second
And go nowhere at all

At times
Time's a funny thing
Time tends to
Escape me…

…I love you—
Don't get me wrong.
I just think it's pretty shitty
When you turn our world
Upside down.

So, can you do me a favor?

Next time,
When you're around,
Invent something to make us rich

Video Talk

I could just let it all go
Because I find all the beauty I need,
When I lean
My ear
To my brother's heart
And I hear
His video talk,
Like a murmur through the ailing
Vent,
When people vent out loud
To each other
Only,
This murmur makes me smile,
And I find all the beauty I need.

To a Lover

The contagious qualities
Of your smile it
Makes me smile all the same
You make me privileged to
Be around you,
Privileged to know your name

Your name means to me,
No one can Love like God can
But when it comes to you and me
It comes pretty close
You make me come alive
You inspire all my poetry

My poetry imitates
Your energy you emit into
The world around us

In Wisconsin

When women Live in
Wisconsin in the winter they become
Super

When she drives into a snowbank she'll do
Anything and everything
Before calling for help and
When help never comes,
She takes matters into her
Own hands

Relies on her own two feet saying
God I got too caught up in
Being super and I know it's been
Too long but
I don't have Time to be scared
I take my church with me I
Know you're always with me and
If my feet don't fail me I
Know it's because
YOU
Made me

Real Love

I never feel smaller than
When I'm missing you
Probably because of how
Small I felt when I was
With you when we
Spent Time together you
Tried to undermine my
Abilities—me being trusting
I started to believe you
Not yet realizing you
Weren't in a place to be
Trusted with my Trust
With my touch
With my Love

Now I'm beginning to know
Just how tall I am
Just how wide the span of my
Arms is just how
Far the reach of my
Voice is

I don't want anymore
Relationships shorter than
Vine vids anymore

You helped me know this
The next Time I take that
Same kind of risk
I'll have the courage and the
Know-how to
Never hesitate
And to realize
When it's real Love
It'll never be too late

Like a Light

In the depths of my psyche
Way in the back
There's a room
And the light is on
But no one's home

I enter the room
I feel foreign
Like I don't belong here
I sit on the plush couch anyway
Waiting for something to happen
Waiting for someone to enter

Then realize
This space is my secret place
A place where it's an honor to be invited
While undiscovered territory
Maybe this room is the realm of getting to
Know who I am
I'll let you know when I find out

Premise

Women are trapped into thinking
They need to have
The premise of their lives
Figured out
By a certain age

Well, to that I say,
Is the mothering of a child
Something to take lightly?
That if I'm not so sure about that
That I should feel behind when
I'm really right where
I'm supposed to be?
Because to me,
Child-bearing is for when I'm 110% sure
And I may never reach that point

It went better than I thought when I
Told my mom
I might never have kids
I was expecting her home to crumble around us
Instead she just said
"Okay"

In this moment
I felt truly seen
Because the premise of my life
Is only beginning
I don't have to have it all figured out
I think I'll just go out and about
Over the mountains and through the hills

We

Look into my weary eyes
I see all your pain
All your potential
When it's scary to walk
On a road alone, I hope
You can remember
With one of you—there's
Only one of you, but add me
Then we have
We

Sometimes we just need a
Friend we can
Rest our
Teary eyes with
'Cause tears held in for
So long you don't even know
Where to begin to
Begin to understand
The root of it all
Ultimately turns into
Heart disease
And like the words from Queen Bey
It's the soul that needs the surgery

Look into my weary eyes
Right here, right now,
I see your perfection.
I see your personality
Strong, first and foremost, diligent
Resilient and
Sweet as a confection
I see your heart beating
To the rhythm sending
Secret messages meant for
The revolution
I see your body a
Manifestation of the part of
God that Lives in you that
Helps you Live out your part
In being part of God

If to Love another person
Is to see the face of God
When I see your face
I see The Universe
An every expanding vessel of
Love

Rest your teary eyes
I'll cry alone with you
Lend you a landscape of a
Warm shoulder to lean on the
Black hole of my ears I

Hear everything you're saying I
Listen to strive to understand and
Your secrets enter
Through a one-way portal
Back to the Universe
Everyone needs a main one
They tell all their secrets to
A ride or die, a true connection
Safe to be vulnerable in

Everyone needs a main one
Someone they can tell all their
Secrets to
I'm here volunteering to
Be that for you

Please remember

With you alone, there's,
Just one you, but, add me
And now we have we
In my heart, mind and eyes
You'll always have—WE

A Poet's Poem

If I didn't write
I'd be locked up
If I decided there was no
Time
I'd lose my damn mind
Because keeping these thoughts
To just roam free
To allow these feelings I'm feeling to remain
inside
In some type of way
My sanity would die

Tie-dyed shirts and
Faded dreams
Writing helps me see
My dreams
Some ethereal seemingly impossible
Nothing becomes tangible
That's the thing
That's the key

To think what I think
To feel what I feel
And to be able to see it
To determine if it's sane or not

If I didn't write, I'd be locked up
Because like that J. Cole quote
I know deep down every poet
Just wants to be loved